Hearts Are Everywhere

A 52-Week Devotional Journal by Lela Rast Hartsaw

This Journal Belongs To

WhatsMamaWriting Press
2022

Dedication & Thanks

This journal is dedicated to the man I am so grateful for: my husband, Mike Hartsaw, who is my loving, supportive lobster.

Special thanks goes to my kiddos, Emily & David, who are amazingly understanding when their mama needs to spend hours of "seat time" while working on a book.

Copyright ©2022 by Lela Rast Hartsaw
WhatsMamaWriting Press

ISBN 978-1-7369652-1-4

Printed in the United States of America
(Unless purchased outside the USA.)

Book design by Lela Rast Hartsaw
Contact the author by email:
whatsmamawriting@gmail.com

How to use this book:

If you keep an eye out, you'll see hearts are indeed everywhere. Finding a heart at the beach, or in the grocery store parking lot, or perhaps in your salad at lunch can be a simple reminder of the love that surrounds you.

This journal was inspired by my collection of photos of the hearts I have found in unexpected places and was created as a weekly tool with:

- Daily schedule boxes for week-at-a-glance notes and reminders
- A Bible verse each week — a collection of verses from Genesis to Revelation showing a sampling of God's Word regarding LOVE
- Space to reflect on the week's Bible verse and what it means to you
- A check list to fill with priorities and check them off as you go
- An inspirational quote on LOVE from famous people past & present
- Weekly Habit Tracker to keep up with personal goals
- The grid paper is an invitation to make a journal entry using words, doodles, affixed mementos, decorative stickers or tape, rubber-stamped images... It's a space to do whatever inspires you

You can follow @Hearts.Everywhere.Journal on Instagram to see the hearts I've discovered. I hope my collection of heart photos encourages you to look for them in your day-to-day life, too, and I hope this 52-week devotional journal is useful and brings you joy.

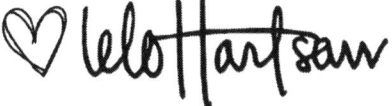

PS. Choosing a black & white interior for this book kept the printing cost low so that this journal could make an easy, thoughtful gift or perhaps be used as a fundraiser for your small group or organization.

monday

WEEKLY Bible Verse

This is the reason man leaves his father & mother and embraces his wife, and they become one flesh.

GENESIS 2:24

tuesday

wednesday

What's it mean?
TO ME THIS VERSE SAYS:

thursday

friday

saturday / sunday

Instagram
@HEARTS.
EVERYWHERE.
JOURNAL

Write it down. Check it off!

> "What we have once enjoyed we can never lose. All that we love deeply becomes part of us."
>
> —HELEN KELLER

habit TRACKER M T W T F S S

| JAN | FEB | MAR | APR | MAY | JUN | JUL | AUG | SEP | OCT | NOV | DEC |

1 2 3 4 5 6 7 8 9 10 11 12 13 14 15 16 17 18 19 20 21 22 23 24 25 26 27 28 29 30 31

monday

tuesday

wednesday

thursday

friday

saturday / sunday

Weekly Bible Verse

Give thanks to the Lord, for He is good, His love endures forever.

1 CHRONICLES 16:34

What's it mean?

TO ME THIS VERSE SAYS:

Instagram
@HEARTS.
EVERYWHERE.
JOURNAL

✓ *Write it down. Check it off!*

> Loved you yesterday, love you still, always have, always will.
>
> —ELAINE DAVIS

habit TRACKER

	M	T	W	T	F	S	S
___	○	○	○	○	○	○	○
___	○	○	○	○	○	○	○
___	○	○	○	○	○	○	○
___	○	○	○	○	○	○	○
___	○	○	○	○	○	○	○

JAN	FEB	MAR	APR	MAY	JUN	JUL	AUG	SEP	OCT	NOV	DEC

1 2 3 4 5 6 7 8 9 10 11 12 13 14 15 16 17 18 19 20 21 22 23 24 25 26 27 28 29 30 31

monday

tuesday

wednesday

WEEKLY Bible Verse

You clothed me with skin and flesh, and knit me together with bones and sinews. You have granted me life and steadfast love, and your care has preserved my spirit.

JOB 10:11-12

thursday

friday

What's it mean?
TO ME THIS VERSE SAYS:

saturday / sunday

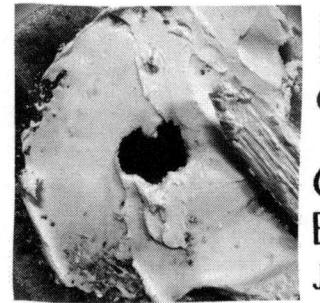

Instagram
@HEARTS.
EVERYWHERE.
JOURNAL

✓ *Write it down. Check it off!*

> "You, yourself, as much as anybody in the entire universe, deserve your love and affection."
>
> —BUDDHA

habit TRACKER M T W T F S S

| JAN | FEB | MAR | APR | MAY | JUN | JUL | AUG | SEP | OCT | NOV | DEC |

1 2 3 4 5 6 7 8 9 10 11 12 13 14 15 16 17 18 19 20 21 22 23 24 25 26 27 28 29 30 31

monday

tuesday

wednesday

thursday

friday

saturday / sunday

WEEKLY
Bible Verse

Have mercy on me, O God, according to your unfailing love; according to your great compassion blot out my transgressions.

PSALM 51:1

What's it mean?
TO ME THIS VERSE SAYS:

Instagram
@HEARTS.
EVERYWHERE.
JOURNAL

✓ *Write it down. Check it off!*

> "We loved with a love that was more than love."
> —EDGAR ALLAN POE

habit TRACKER — M T W T F S S

| JAN | FEB | MAR | APR | MAY | JUN | JUL | AUG | SEP | OCT | NOV | DEC |

1 2 3 4 5 6 7 8 9 10 11 12 13 14 15 16 17 18 19 20 21 22 23 24 25 26 27 28 29 30 31

monday

tuesday

wednesday

But you, Lord, are a compassionate and gracious God, slow to anger, abounding in love and faithfulness.

PSALM 86:15

thursday

friday

What's it mean?
TO ME THIS VERSE SAYS:

saturday / sunday

Instagram
@HEARTS.
EVERYWHERE.
JOURNAL

Write it down. Check it off!

> One is loved because one is loved.
> No reason is needed for loving.
>
> —PAULO COELHO

habit TRACKER

	M	T	W	T	F	S	S
_____	○	○	○	○	○	○	○
_____	○	○	○	○	○	○	○
_____	○	○	○	○	○	○	○
_____	○	○	○	○	○	○	○
_____	○	○	○	○	○	○	○

| JAN | FEB | MAR | APR | MAY | JUN | JUL | AUG | SEP | OCT | NOV | DEC |

1 2 3 4 5 6 7 8 9 10 11 12 13 14 15 16 17 18 19 20 21 22 23 24 25 26 27 28 29 30 31

monday

WEEKLY Bible Verse

Let the morning bring me word of your unfailing love, for I have put my trust in you. Show me the way I should go, for to you I entrust my life.

PSALM 143:8

tuesday

wednesday

What's it mean?
TO ME THIS VERSE SAYS:

thursday

friday

saturday / sunday

Instagram
@HEARTS.
EVERYWHERE.
JOURNAL

Write it down. Check it off!

> "Love is shown more in deeds than in words."
> —SAINT IGNATIUS

habit TRACKER M T W T F S S

| JAN | FEB | MAR | APR | MAY | JUN | JUL | AUG | SEP | OCT | NOV | DEC |

2 3 4 5 6 7 8 9 10 11 12 13 14 15 16 17 18 19 20 21 22 23 24 25 26 27 28 29 30 31

monday

tuesday

wednesday

He heals the broken-hearted and binds up their wounds.

PSALM 147:3

thursday

friday

What's it mean?
TO ME THIS VERSE SAYS:

saturday / sunday

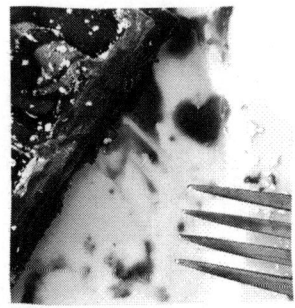

Instagram
@HEARTS.
EVERYWHERE.
JOURNAL

✓ *Write it down. Check it off!*

> Being deeply loved by someone gives you strength, while loving someone deeply gives you courage.
>
> —LAU TZU

habit TRACKER — M T W T F S S

| JAN | FEB | MAR | APR | MAY | JUN | JUL | AUG | SEP | OCT | NOV | DEC |

1 2 3 4 5 6 7 8 9 10 11 12 13 14 15 16 17 18 19 20 21 22 23 24 25 26 27 28 29 30 31

WEEKLY Bible Verse

- monday
- tuesday
- wednesday
- thursday
- friday
- saturday / sunday

Let love and faithfulness never leave you; bind them around your neck, write them on the tablet in your heart. Then you will win favor and a good name in the sight of God and man.

PROVERBS 3:3-4

What's it mean?
TO ME THIS VERSE SAYS:

Instagram
@HEARTS.EVERYWHERE.JOURNAL

Write it down. Check it off!

> Love is that condition in which the happiness of another is essential to your own.
>
> —ROBERT H. HEINLEIN

habit TRACKER

	M	T	W	T	F	S	S
___	○	○	○	○	○	○	○
___	○	○	○	○	○	○	○
___	○	○	○	○	○	○	○
___	○	○	○	○	○	○	○
___	○	○	○	○	○	○	○

| JAN | FEB | MAR | APR | MAY | JUN | JUL | AUG | SEP | OCT | NOV | DEC |

1　2　3　4　5　6　7　8　9　10　11　12　13　14　15　16　17　18　19　20　21　22　23　24　25　26　27　28　29　30　31

monday

tuesday

wednesday

Above all else, guard your heart, for everything you do flows from it.

PROVERBS 4:23

thursday

friday

What's it mean?
TO ME THIS VERSE SAYS:

saturday / sunday

Instagram
@HEARTS.
EVERYWHERE.
JOURNAL

✓ **Write it down. Check it off!**

> "I think... if it is true that there are as many minds as there are heads, then there are as many kinds of love as there are hearts.
>
> —LEO TOLSTOY"

habit TRACKER

	M	T	W	T	F	S	S
_____	○	○	○	○	○	○	○
_____	○	○	○	○	○	○	○
_____	○	○	○	○	○	○	○
_____	○	○	○	○	○	○	○
_____	○	○	○	○	○	○	○

| JAN | FEB | MAR | APR | MAY | JUN | JUL | AUG | SEP | OCT | NOV | DEC |

1 2 3 4 5 6 7 8 9 10 11 12 13 14 15 16 17 18 19 20 21 22 23 24 25 26 27 28 29 30 31

monday

tuesday

wednesday

I love those who love me,
those who seek me will find me.

PROVERBS 8:17

thursday

friday

What's it mean?
TO ME THIS VERSE SAYS:

saturday / sunday

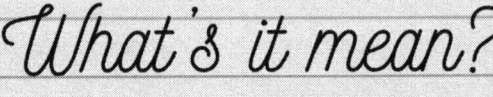

@HEARTS.
EVERYWHERE.
JOURNAL

Write it down. Check it off!

> "Love is like the wind, you can't see it, but you can feel it."
>
> —NICHOLAS SPARKS

habit TRACKER — M T W T F S S

| JAN | FEB | MAR | APR | MAY | JUN | JUL | AUG | SEP | OCT | NOV | DEC |

1 2 3 4 5 6 7 8 9 10 11 12 13 14 15 16 17 18 19 20 21 22 23 24 25 26 27 28 29 30 31

monday

tuesday

wednesday

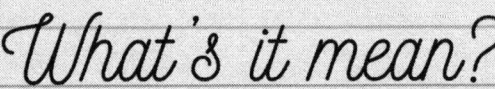

Hatred stirs up conflict, but love covers over all wrongs.

PROVERBS 10:12

thursday

friday

What's it mean?
TO ME THIS VERSE SAYS:

saturday / sunday

Instagram
@HEARTS.
EVERYWHERE.
JOURNAL

Write it down. Check it off!

> "Love is all you need. But a little chocolate, now and then, doesn't hurt."
>
> —CHARLES M. SHULZ

habit TRACKER M T W T F S S

| JAN | FEB | MAR | APR | MAY | JUN | JUL | AUG | SEP | OCT | NOV | DEC |

1 2 3 4 5 6 7 8 9 10 11 12 13 14 15 16 17 18 19 20 21 22 23 24 25 26 27 28 29 30 31

WEEKLY Bible Verse

monday

tuesday

wednesday

thursday

friday

saturday / sunday

A friend loves at all times, and a brother is born for adversity.

PROVERBS 17:17

What's it mean?
TO ME THIS VERSE SAYS:

Instagram
@HEARTS.EVERYWHERE.JOURNAL

Write it down. Check it off!

> "There is always madness in love. But there is also always some reason in madness."
>
> —FRIEDRICH NIETSCHE

habit TRACKER M T W T F S S

| JAN | FEB | MAR | APR | MAY | JUN | JUL | AUG | SEP | OCT | NOV | DEC |

1 2 3 4 5 6 7 8 9 10 11 12 13 14 15 16 17 18 19 20 21 22 23 24 25 26 27 28 29 30 31

monday

tuesday

wednesday

House and wealth are inherited from fathers, but a prudent wife is from the Lord.

PROVERBS 19:14

thursday

friday

What's it mean?
TO ME THIS VERSE SAYS:

saturday / sunday

Instagram
@HEARTS.
EVERYWHERE.
JOURNAL

Write it down Check it off!

> You know it's love when all you want is that person to be happy, even if you're not part of their happiness.
>
> —JULIA ROBERTS

habit TRACKER

M T W T F S S

| JAN | FEB | MAR | APR | MAY | JUN | JUL | AUG | SEP | OCT | NOV | DEC |

1 2 3 4 5 6 7 8 9 10 11 12 13 14 15 16 17 18 19 20 21 22 23 24 25 26 27 28 29 30 31

monday

tuesday

wednesday

WEEKLY Bible Verse

Whoever pursues righteousness and love finds life, prosperity, and honor.

PROVERBS 21:21

thursday

friday

What's it mean?
TO ME THIS VERSE SAYS:

saturday / sunday

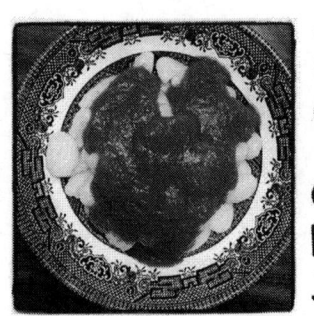

Instagram
@HEARTS.
EVERYWHERE.
JOURNAL

✓ *Write it down. Check it off!*

> "Have enough courage to trust love one more time and always one more time."
>
> —MAYA ANGELOU

habit TRACKER — M T W T F S S

| JAN | FEB | MAR | APR | MAY | JUN | JUL | AUG | SEP | OCT | NOV | DEC |

1 2 3 4 5 6 7 8 9 10 11 12 13 14 15 16 17 18 19 20 21 22 23 24 25 26 27 28 29 30 31

Weekly Bible Verse

monday

tuesday

wednesday

thursday

friday

saturday / sunday

An excellent wife who can find? She is far more precious than jewels.

PROVERBS 31:10

What's it mean?
TO ME THIS VERSE SAYS:

Instagram
@HEARTS.
EVERYWHERE.
JOURNAL

Write it down. Check it off!

- [x]
- [ ]
- [ ]
- [ ]
- [ ]
- [ ]
- [ ]
- [ ]
- [ ]
- [ ]
- [ ]
- [ ]

> "I love you not for what you are, but for who I am when I am with you."
>
> —ROY CROFT

habit TRACKER

	M	T	W	T	F	S	S
___	○	○	○	○	○	○	○
___	○	○	○	○	○	○	○
___	○	○	○	○	○	○	○
___	○	○	○	○	○	○	○
___	○	○	○	○	○	○	○

JAN	FEB	MAR	APR	MAY	JUN	JUL	AUG	SEP	OCT	NOV	DEC

1 2 3 4 5 6 7 8 9 10 11 12 13 14 15 16 17 18 19 20 21 22 23 24 25 26 27 28 29 30 31

monday

tuesday

wednesday

WEEKLY
Bible Verse

I found the one my heart loves.

SONG OF SOLOMON 3:4

thursday

friday

What's it mean?
TO ME THIS VERSE SAYS:

saturday / sunday

Instagram
@HEARTS.
EVERYWHERE.
JOURNAL

✓ *Write it down. Check it off!*

> When you realize you want to spend the rest of your life with somebody, you want the rest of your life to start as soon as possible.
>
> —NORA EPHRON
> (WHEN HARRY MET SALLY)

habit TRACKER

M T W T F S S

| JAN | FEB | MAR | APR | MAY | JUN | JUL | AUG | SEP | OCT | NOV | DEC |

1 2 3 4 5 6 7 8 9 10 11 12 13 14 15 16 17 18 19 20 21 22 23 24 25 26 27 28 29 30 31

WEEKLY Bible Verse

monday

tuesday

wednesday

thursday

friday

saturday / sunday

I am my beloved's and my beloved is mine.

SONG OF SOLOMON 8:3

What's it mean?
TO ME THIS VERSE SAYS:

Instagram
@HEARTS.
EVERYWHERE.
JOURNAL

✓ Write it down. Check it off!

> "Whatever our souls are made of, his and mine are the same.
>
> —EMILY BRONTE"

habit TRACKER M T W T F S S

| JAN | FEB | MAR | APR | MAY | JUN | JUL | AUG | SEP | OCT | NOV | DEC |

1 2 3 4 5 6 7 8 9 10 11 12 13 14 15 16 17 18 19 20 21 22 23 24 25 26 27 28 29 30 31

monday

tuesday

wednesday

thursday

friday

saturday / sunday

I have loved you with an everlasting love; I have drawn you with unfailing kindness.

JEREMIAH 31:3

What's it mean?
TO ME THIS VERSE SAYS:

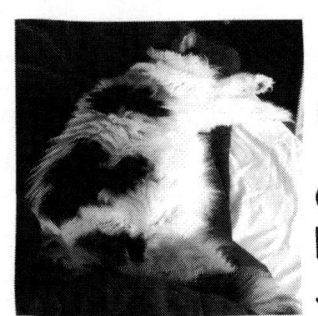

Instagram
@HEARTS.
EVERYWHERE.
JOURNAL

Write it down. Check it off!

> "Love is the whole thing.
> We are only pieces."
> —RUMI

habit TRACKER — M T W T F S S

| JAN | FEB | MAR | APR | MAY | JUN | JUL | AUG | SEP | OCT | NOV | DEC |

1 2 3 4 5 6 7 8 9 10 11 12 13 14 15 16 17 18 19 20 21 22 23 24 25 26 27 28 29 30 31

monday

tuesday

wednesday

WEEKLY Bible Verse

And I will betroth you to me forever. I will betroth you to me in righteousness and justice, in steadfast love and in mercy.

HOSEA 2:19

thursday

friday

What's it mean?
TO ME THIS VERSE SAYS:

saturday / sunday

Instagram
@HEARTS.
EVERYWHERE.
JOURNAL

✓ *Write it down. Check it off!*

> To love and be loved is to feel the sun from both sides.
>
> —DAVID VISCOTT

habit TRACKER — M T W T F S S

| JAN | FEB | MAR | APR | MAY | JUN | JUL | AUG | SEP | OCT | NOV | DEC |

1 2 3 4 5 6 7 8 9 10 11 12 13 14 15 16 17 18 19 20 21 22 23 24 25 26 27 28 29 30 31

monday

tuesday

wednesday

thursday

friday

saturday / sunday

WEEKLY Bible Verse

He has shown you, O mortal, what is good. And what does the Lord require of you? To act justly and to love mercy and to walk humbly with your God.

MICAH 6:8

What's it mean?
TO ME THIS VERSE SAYS:

Instagram
@HEARTS.
EVERYWHERE.
JOURNAL

✓ *Write it down. Check it off!*

> "Life is the flower for which love is the honey."
> —VICTOR HUGO

habit TRACKER

	M	T	W	T	F	S	S
_____	○	○	○	○	○	○	○
_____	○	○	○	○	○	○	○
_____	○	○	○	○	○	○	○
_____	○	○	○	○	○	○	○
_____	○	○	○	○	○	○	○

| JAN | FEB | MAR | APR | MAY | JUN | JUL | AUG | SEP | OCT | NOV | DEC |

1 2 3 4 5 6 7 8 9 10 11 12 13 14 15 16 17 18 19 20 21 22 23 24 25 26 27 28 29 30 31

monday

tuesday

wednesday

thursday

friday

saturday / sunday

Weekly Bible Verse

No one can serve two masters. Either you will hate one and love the other, or you will be loyal to the one and have contempt for the other.

MATTHEW 6:24

What's it mean?
TO ME THIS VERSE SAYS:

Instagram
@HEARTS.
EVERYWHERE.
JOURNAL

✓ *Write it down. Check it off!*

> "You always gain by giving love.
>
> —REESE WITHERSPOON"

habit TRACKER

	M	T	W	T	F	S	S
_____	○	○	○	○	○	○	○
_____	○	○	○	○	○	○	○
_____	○	○	○	○	○	○	○
_____	○	○	○	○	○	○	○
_____	○	○	○	○	○	○	○

| JAN | FEB | MAR | APR | MAY | JUN | JUL | AUG | SEP | OCT | NOV | DEC |

1 2 3 4 5 6 7 8 9 10 11 12 13 14 15 16 17 18 19 20 21 22 23 24 25 26 27 28 29 30 31

monday

tuesday

wednesday

thursday

friday

saturday / sunday

"Teacher, what is the greatest law?" He replied, "You must love the Lord your God with all your heart, with all your being, and with all your mind. This is the first and greatest commandment. And the second is like it. You must love your neighbor as you love yourself. All the Law and the Prophets depend on these two commands."

MATTHEW 22:36-40

What's it mean?

TO ME THIS VERSE SAYS:

Instagram
@HEARTS.
EVERYWHERE.
JOURNAL

Write it down. Check it off!

> "Love is composed of a single soul in habiting two bodies."
> —ARISTOTLE

habit TRACKER — M T W T F S S

| JAN | FEB | MAR | APR | MAY | JUN | JUL | AUG | SEP | OCT | NOV | DEC |

1 2 3 4 5 6 7 8 9 10 11 12 13 14 15 16 17 18 19 20 21 22 23 24 25 26 27 28 29 30 31

monday

tuesday

wednesday

Therefore what God has joined together, let no one separate.

MARK 10:9

thursday

friday

What's it mean?
TO ME THIS VERSE SAYS:

saturday / sunday

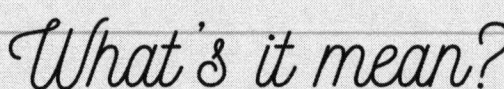

Instagram
@HEARTS.
EVERYWHERE.
JOURNAL

✓ Write it down. Check it off!

> "We are the most alive when we are in love."
> —JOHN UPDIKE

habit TRACKER — M T W T F S S

| JAN | FEB | MAR | APR | MAY | JUN | JUL | AUG | SEP | OCT | NOV | DEC |

1 2 3 4 5 6 7 8 9 10 11 12 13 14 15 16 17 18 19 20 21 22 23 24 25 26 27 28 29 30 31

monday

tuesday

wednesday

But to you who are listening I say: Love your enemies, do good to those who hate you, bless those that curse you, pray for those who mistreat you.

LUKE 6:27

thursday

friday

What's it mean?
TO ME THIS VERSE SAYS:

saturday / sunday

Instagram
@HEARTS.
EVERYWHERE.
JOURNAL

✓ *Write it down. Check it off!*

> "There is no charm equal to tenderness of the heart."
>
> —JANE AUSTEN

habit TRACKER — M T W T F S S

| JAN | FEB | MAR | APR | MAY | JUN | JUL | AUG | SEP | OCT | NOV | DEC |

1 2 3 4 5 6 7 8 9 10 11 12 13 14 15 16 17 18 19 20 21 22 23 24 25 26 27 28 29 30 31

monday

tuesday

wednesday

WEEKLY Bible Verse

Do to others as you would have them do to you.

LUKE 6:31

What's it mean?
TO ME THIS VERSE SAYS:

thursday

friday

saturday / sunday

Instagram
@HEARTS.
EVERYWHERE.
JOURNAL

✓ *Write it down Check it off!*

> "The heart has its reasons of which reason knows nothing.
>
> —BLAISE PASCAL"

habit TRACKER — M T W T F S S

| JAN | FEB | MAR | APR | MAY | JUN | JUL | AUG | SEP | OCT | NOV | DEC |

1 2 3 4 5 6 7 8 9 10 11 12 13 14 15 16 17 18 19 20 21 22 23 24 25 26 27 28 29 30 31

monday

tuesday

wednesday

> God so loved the world that he gave his only son, so that whoever believes in Him will not perish, but have eternal life.
>
> JOHN 3:16

thursday

friday

What's it mean?
TO ME THIS VERSE SAYS:

saturday / sunday

Instagram
@HEARTS.
EVERYWHERE.
JOURNAL

✓ *Write it down. Check it off!*

> "Love is a friendship that has caught fire."
>
> —ANN LANDERS

habit TRACKER M T W T F S S

| JAN | FEB | MAR | APR | MAY | JUN | JUL | AUG | SEP | OCT | NOV | DEC |

1 2 3 4 5 6 7 8 9 10 11 12 13 14 15 16 17 18 19 20 21 22 23 24 25 26 27 28 29 30 31

monday

tuesday

wednesday

thursday

friday

saturday / sunday

WEEKLY Bible Verse

My command is this: Love each other as I have loved you.

JOHN 15:12

What's it mean?

TO ME THIS VERSE SAYS:

Instagram
@HEARTS.EVERYWHERE.JOURNAL

Write it down. Check it off!

> Love yourself first and everything else falls into line.
>
> —LUCILLE BALL

habit TRACKER — M T W T F S S

| JAN | FEB | MAR | APR | MAY | JUN | JUL | AUG | SEP | OCT | NOV | DEC |

1 2 3 4 5 6 7 8 9 10 11 12 13 14 15 16 17 18 19 20 21 22 23 24 25 26 27 28 29 30 31

WEEKLY Bible Verse

monday

tuesday

wednesday

We know that God works all things together for good for the ones who love God, for those who are called according to His purpose.

ROMANS 8:28

thursday

friday

What's it mean?
TO ME THIS VERSE SAYS:

saturday / sunday

Instagram
@HEARTS.
EVERYWHERE.
JOURNAL

Write it down. Check it off!

> "You can't blame gravity for falling in love."
> —ALBERT EINSTEIN

habit TRACKER — M T W T F S S

| JAN | FEB | MAR | APR | MAY | JUN | JUL | AUG | SEP | OCT | NOV | DEC |

1 2 3 4 5 6 7 8 9 10 11 12 13 14 15 16 17 18 19 20 21 22 23 24 25 26 27 28 29 30 31

monday

tuesday

wednesday

WEEKLY
Bible Verse

Love must be sincere. Hate what is evil; cling to what is good.

ROMANS 12:9

thursday

friday

What's it mean?
TO ME THIS VERSE SAYS:

saturday / sunday

Instagram
@HEARTS.
EVERYWHERE.
JOURNAL

✓ *Write it down. Check it off!*

> "If you find someone you love in your life, then hang on to that love."
>
> —PRINCESS DIANA

habit TRACKER — M T W T F S S

| JAN | FEB | MAR | APR | MAY | JUN | JUL | AUG | SEP | OCT | NOV | DEC |

1 2 3 4 5 6 7 8 9 10 11 12 13 14 15 16 17 18 19 20 21 22 23 24 25 26 27 28 29 30 31

monday

tuesday

wednesday

Let no debt remain outstanding, except the continuing debt to love one another, for whoever loves others has fulfilled the law.

ROMANS 13:8

thursday

friday

What's it mean?
TO ME THIS VERSE SAYS:

saturday / sunday

Instagram
@HEARTS.
EVERYWHERE.
JOURNAL

✓ *Write it down. Check it off!*

> "I fell in love the way you fall asleep: slowly, and then all at once.
>
> —JOHN GREEN"

habit TRACKER M T W T F S S

| JAN | FEB | MAR | APR | MAY | JUN | JUL | AUG | SEP | OCT | NOV | DEC |

1 2 3 4 5 6 7 8 9 10 11 12 13 14 15 16 17 18 19 20 21 22 23 24 25 26 27 28 29 30 31

monday

tuesday

wednesday

thursday

friday

saturday / sunday

If I have the gift of prophecy and can fathom all the mysteries and all knowledge, and I have faith that can move mountains, but I do not have love, I am nothing.

1 CORINTHIANS 13:2

What's it mean?
TO ME THIS VERSE SAYS:

Instagram
@HEARTS.
EVERYWHERE.
JOURNAL

✓ *Write it down Check it off!*

> "If you live to be a hundred, I want to live to be a hundred minus one day, so I never have to live without you."
>
> —WINNIE THE POOH

habit TRACKER M T W T F S S

| JAN | FEB | MAR | APR | MAY | JUN | JUL | AUG | SEP | OCT | NOV | DEC |

1 2 3 4 5 6 7 8 9 10 11 12 13 14 15 16 17 18 19 20 21 22 23 24 25 26 27 28 29 30 31

monday

tuesday

wednesday

thursday

friday

saturday / sunday

Love is patient and kind. It is never jealous. Love is never boastful or conceited. It is never rude or selfish. It does not take offense and is not resentful. Love takes no pleasure in other people's sins, but delights in the truth. It is always ready to excuse, to trust, to hope, and to endure whatever comes.

1 CORINTHIANS 13:4-7

What's it mean?
TO ME THIS VERSE SAYS:

Instagram
@HEARTS.
EVERYWHERE.
JOURNAL

Write it down. Check it off!

> "It is better to have loved and lost than never to have loved at all."
>
> —ALFRED LORD TENNYSON

habit TRACKER — M T W T F S S

| JAN | FEB | MAR | APR | MAY | JUN | JUL | AUG | SEP | OCT | NOV | DEC |

1 2 3 4 5 6 7 8 9 10 11 12 13 14 15 16 17 18 19 20 21 22 23 24 25 26 27 28 29 30 31

monday

tuesday

wednesday

And now these three remain:
faith, hope, and love.
But the greatest of these is love.

1 CORINTHIANS 13:13

thursday

friday

What's it mean?
TO ME THIS VERSE SAYS:

saturday / sunday

Instagram
@HEARTS.
EVERYWHERE.
JOURNAL

Write it down. Check it off!

> "We're born alone, we live alone, we die alone. Only through our love and friendship can we create the illusion for a moment that we are not alone."
>
> —ORSON WELLES

habit TRACKER

	M	T	W	T	F	S	S
_____	○	○	○	○	○	○	○
_____	○	○	○	○	○	○	○
_____	○	○	○	○	○	○	○
_____	○	○	○	○	○	○	○
_____	○	○	○	○	○	○	○

| JAN | FEB | MAR | APR | MAY | JUN | JUL | AUG | SEP | OCT | NOV | DEC |

1 2 3 4 5 6 7 8 9 10 11 12 13 14 15 16 17 18 19 20 21 22 23 24 25 26 27 28 29 30 31

WEEKLY Bible Verse

- monday
- tuesday
- wednesday
- thursday
- friday
- saturday / sunday

Do everything in love.

1 CORINTHIANS 16:14

What's it mean?
TO ME THIS VERSE SAYS:

Instagram
@HEARTS.EVERYWHERE.JOURNAL

Write it down Check it off!

> "Let us always meet each other with a smile, for the smile is hte beginning of love."
>
> —MOTHER TERESA

habit TRACKER M T W T F S S

| JAN | FEB | MAR | APR | MAY | JUN | JUL | AUG | SEP | OCT | NOV | DEC |

1 2 3 4 5 6 7 8 9 10 11 12 13 14 15 16 17 18 19 20 21 22 23 24 25 26 27 28 29 30 31

monday

tuesday
wednesday

WEEKLY
Bible Verse

The entire law is fulfilled in keeping this one command: Love your neighbor as yourself.

GALATIANS 5:13

thursday
friday

What's it mean?
TO ME THIS VERSE SAYS:

saturday / sunday

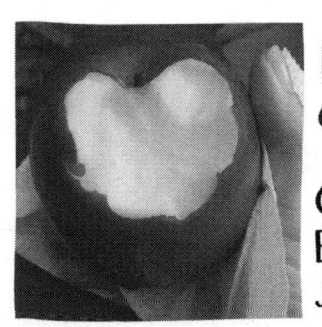

Instagram
@HEARTS.
EVERYWHERE.
JOURNAL

✓ Write it down Check it off!

> "Time is too slow for those who wait, too swift for those who fear, too long for those who grieve, too short for those who rejoice, but for those who love, time is eternity.
> —HENRY VAN DYKE"

habit TRACKER M T W T F S S

| JAN | FEB | MAR | APR | MAY | JUN | JUL | AUG | SEP | OCT | NOV | DEC |

1 2 3 4 5 6 7 8 9 10 11 12 13 14 15 16 17 18 19 20 21 22 23 24 25 26 27 28 29 30 31

monday

tuesday

wednesday

thursday

friday

saturday / sunday

Weekly Bible Verse

Be completely humble and gentle; be patient, bearing with one another in love.

EPHESIANS 4:2

What's it mean?
TO ME THIS VERSE SAYS:

Instagram
@HEARTS.
EVERYWHERE.
JOURNAL

Write it down Check it off!

> True love is like ghosts, which everyone talks about and few have seen.
>
> —FRANCOIS DE LA ROCHEFOUCAULD

habit TRACKER M T W T F S S

| JAN | FEB | MAR | APR | MAY | JUN | JUL | AUG | SEP | OCT | NOV | DEC |

1 2 3 4 5 6 7 8 9 10 11 12 13 14 15 16 17 18 19 20 21 22 23 24 25 26 27 28 29 30 31

monday

tuesday

wednesday

Be kind, compassionate, and forgiving to each other, in the same way God forgave you in Christ.

EPHESIANS 4:32

thursday

friday

What's it mean?
TO ME THIS VERSE SAYS:

saturday / sunday

Instagram
@HEARTS.
EVERYWHERE.
JOURNAL

✓ *Write it down Check it off!*

> "Where there is love, there is life.
> —MAHATMA GANDHI"

habit TRACKER — M T W T F S S

| JAN | FEB | MAR | APR | MAY | JUN | JUL | AUG | SEP | OCT | NOV | DEC |

1 2 3 4 5 6 7 8 9 10 11 12 13 14 15 16 17 18 19 20 21 22 23 24 25 26 27 28 29 30 31

monday

WEEKLY Bible Verse

As for husbands, love your wives just like Christ loved the church and gave himself to her.

EPHESIANS 5:25

tuesday

wednesday

What's it mean?
TO ME THIS VERSE SAYS:

thursday

friday

saturday / sunday

Instagram
@HEARTS.
EVERYWHERE.
JOURNAL

✓ *Write it down. Check it off!*

> "I feel that there is nothing truly more artistic than to love people.
>
> —VINCENT VAN GOGH"

habit TRACKER — M T W T F S S

| JAN | FEB | MAR | APR | MAY | JUN | JUL | AUG | SEP | OCT | NOV | DEC |

1 2 3 4 5 6 7 8 9 10 11 12 13 14 15 16 17 18 19 20 21 22 23 24 25 26 27 28 29 30 31

monday

tuesday

wednesday

And over all these virtues put on love, which binds them all together in perfect unity.

COLOSSIANS 3:14

thursday

friday

What's it mean?
TO ME THIS VERSE SAYS:

saturday / sunday

Instagram
@HEARTS.
EVERYWHERE.
JOURNAL

✓ *Write it down. Check it off!*

> "Love and compassion are necessities, not luxuries; without them humanity cannot survive.
>
> —DALAI LAMA"

habit TRACKER — M T W T F S S

| JAN | FEB | MAR | APR | MAY | JUN | JUL | AUG | SEP | OCT | NOV | DEC |

1 2 3 4 5 6 7 8 9 10 11 12 13 14 15 16 17 18 19 20 21 22 23 24 25 26 27 28 29 30 31

monday

tuesday

wednesday

thursday

friday

saturday / sunday

Weekly Bible Verse

May the Lord make your love increase and overflow for each other and for everyone else, just as ours does for you.

1 THESSALONIANS 3:12

What's it mean?
TO ME THIS VERSE SAYS:

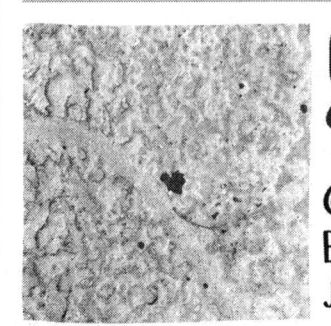

Instagram
@HEARTS.
EVERYWHERE.
JOURNAL

Write it down Check it off!

> "Life without love is like a tree without blossoms or fruit."
>
> —KHALIL GIBRAN

habit TRACKER M T W T F S S

| JAN | FEB | MAR | APR | MAY | JUN | JUL | AUG | SEP | OCT | NOV | DEC |

1 2 3 4 5 6 7 8 9 10 11 12 13 14 15 16 17 18 19 20 21 22 23 24 25 26 27 28 29 30 31

WEEKLY Bible Verse

- monday
- tuesday
- wednesday
- thursday
- friday
- saturday / sunday

May the Lord direct your hearts into God's love and Christ's perseverance.

2 THESSALONIANS 3:5

What's it mean?

TO ME THIS VERSE SAYS:

Instagram
@hearts.everywhere.journal

✓ *Write it down Check it off!*

> "Love is like war: easy to start but very hard to stop."
>
> —H. L. MENCKEN

habit TRACKER M T W T F S S

| JAN | FEB | MAR | APR | MAY | JUN | JUL | AUG | SEP | OCT | NOV | DEC |

1 2 3 4 5 6 7 8 9 10 11 12 13 14 15 16 17 18 19 20 21 22 23 24 25 26 27 28 29 30 31

just LESSONS

monday

tuesday

wednesday

thursday

friday

saturday / sunday

WEEKLY Bible Verse

The purpose of my instruction is that all believers would be filled with love that comes from a pure heart, a clear conscience, and genuine faith.

1 TIMOTHY 1:5

What's it mean?
TO ME THIS VERSE SAYS:

Instagram
@HEARTS.EVERYWHERE.JOURNAL

Write it down. Check it off!

> "True love cannot be found where it does not exist, nor can it be denied where it does."
>
> —TORQUATO TASSO

habit TRACKER

M T W T F S S

| JAN | FEB | MAR | APR | MAY | JUN | JUL | AUG | SEP | OCT | NOV | DEC |

1 2 3 4 5 6 7 8 9 10 11 12 13 14 15 16 17 18 19 20 21 22 23 24 25 26 27 28 29 30 31

monday

tuesday

wednesday

Let us consider how to stir up one another to love and good works.

HEBREWS 10:24

thursday

friday

What's it mean?
TO ME THIS VERSE SAYS:

saturday / sunday

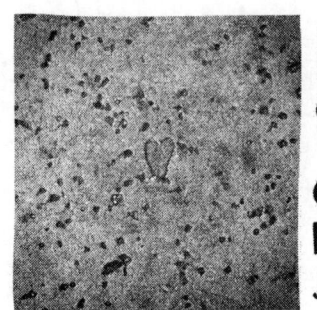

Instagram
@HEARTS.
EVERYWHERE.
JOURNAL

✓ *Write it down Check it off!*

> "Love does not consist of gazing at each other, but looking outward in the same direction."
>
> —ANTOINE DE SAINT-EXUPERY

habit TRACKER

M T W T F S S

| JAN | FEB | MAR | APR | MAY | JUN | JUL | AUG | SEP | OCT | NOV | DEC |

1 2 3 4 5 6 7 8 9 10 11 12 13 14 15 16 17 18 19 20 21 22 23 24 25 26 27 28 29 30 31

monday

tuesday

wednesday

> Keep on loving one another as brothers and sisters. Do not forget to show hospitality to strangers, for by so doing some people have shown hospitality to angels without knowing it.
>
> HEBREWS 13:1-2

thursday

friday

What's it mean?
TO ME THIS VERSE SAYS:

saturday / sunday

Instagram
@HEARTS.
EVERYWHERE.
JOURNAL

✓ *Write it down. Check it off!*

> "To love oneself is the beginning of a lifelong romance."
> —OSCAR WILDE

habit TRACKER — M T W T F S S

| JAN | FEB | MAR | APR | MAY | JUN | JUL | AUG | SEP | OCT | NOV | DEC |

1 2 3 4 5 6 7 8 9 10 11 12 13 14 15 16 17 18 19 20 21 22 23 24 25 26 27 28 29 30 31

monday

tuesday

wednesday

Weekly Bible Verse

Above all, love each other deeply, because love covers over a multitude of sins.

1 PETER 4:8

thursday

friday

What's it mean?
TO ME THIS VERSE SAYS:

saturday / sunday

Instagram
@HEARTS.
EVERYWHERE.
JOURNAL

✓ *Write it down. Check it off!*

> "For small creatures such as we, the vastness is bearable only through love.
>
> —CARL SAGAN"

habit TRACKER

	M	T	W	T	F	S	S
_____	○	○	○	○	○	○	○
_____	○	○	○	○	○	○	○
_____	○	○	○	○	○	○	○
_____	○	○	○	○	○	○	○
_____	○	○	○	○	○	○	○

| JAN | FEB | MAR | APR | MAY | JUN | JUL | AUG | SEP | OCT | NOV | DEC |

1 2 3 4 5 6 7 8 9 10 11 12 13 14 15 16 17 18 19 20 21 22 23 24 25 26 27 28 29 30 31

monday

tuesday

wednesday

WEEKLY
Bible Verse

"Little children, let's not love with words or speech but with action and truth."

1 JOHN 3:18

thursday

friday

What's it mean?
TO ME THIS VERSE SAYS:

saturday / sunday

Instagram
@HEARTS.
EVERYWHERE.
JOURNAL

✓ **Write it down. Check it off!**

> Immature love says, "I love you because I need you." Mature love says, "I need you because I love you."
>
> —ERICH FROMM

habit TRACKER — M T W T F S S

| JAN | FEB | MAR | APR | MAY | JUN | JUL | AUG | SEP | OCT | NOV | DEC |

1 2 3 4 5 6 7 8 9 10 11 12 13 14 15 16 17 18 19 20 21 22 23 24 25 26 27 28 29 30 31

monday

tuesday

wednesday

WEEKLY
Bible Verse

No one has seen God; but if we love one another, God lives in us and His love is made complete in us.

1 JOHN 4:12

thursday

friday

What's it mean?
TO ME THIS VERSE SAYS:

saturday / sunday

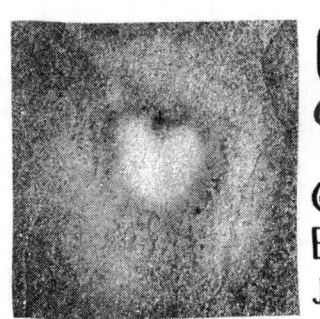

Instagram
@HEARTS.
EVERYWHERE.
JOURNAL

Write it down. Check it off!

> "If you would be loved, love and be loveable."
>
> —BENJAMIN FRANKLIN

habit TRACKER

	M	T	W	T	F	S	S

| JAN | FEB | MAR | APR | MAY | JUN | JUL | AUG | SEP | OCT | NOV | DEC |

1 2 3 4 5 6 7 8 9 10 11 12 13 14 15 16 17 18 19 20 21 22 23 24 25 26 27 28 29 30 31

monday

tuesday

wednesday

WEEKLY Bible Verse

And so we know and rely on the love God has for us. God is love. Whoever lives in love, lives in God, and God in them.

1 JOHN 4:16

thursday

friday

What's it mean?
TO ME THIS VERSE SAYS:

saturday / sunday

Instagram
@HEARTS.EVERYWHERE.JOURNAL

✓ Write it down Check it off!

> Love is a canvas furnished by nature and embroidered by imagination.
> —VOLTAIRE

habit TRACKER — M T W T F S S

| JAN | FEB | MAR | APR | MAY | JUN | JUL | AUG | SEP | OCT | NOV | DEC |

1 2 3 4 5 6 7 8 9 10 11 12 13 14 15 16 17 18 19 20 21 22 23 24 25 26 27 28 29 30 31

monday

tuesday

wednesday

thursday

friday

saturday / sunday

And this is love:
That we walk in obedience to his commands.

2 JOHN 1:6

What's it mean?
TO ME THIS VERSE SAYS:

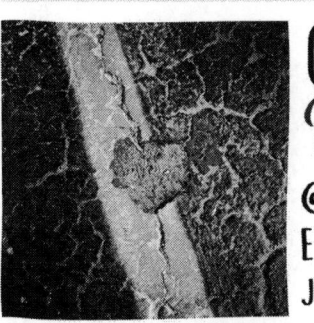

Instagram
@HEARTS.
EVERYWHERE.
JOURNAL

✓ *Write it down. Check it off!*

> "Who so loves believes the impossible.
> —ELIZABETH BARRETT BROWNING"

habit TRACKER — M T W T F S S

| JAN | FEB | MAR | APR | MAY | JUN | JUL | AUG | SEP | OCT | NOV | DEC |

1 2 3 4 5 6 7 8 9 10 11 12 13 14 15 16 17 18 19 20 21 22 23 24 25 26 27 28 29 30 31

monday

May mercy, peace, and love be multiplied to you.

JUDE 1:2

tuesday

wednesday

What's it mean?
TO ME THIS VERSE SAYS:

thursday

friday

saturday / sunday

Instagram
@HEARTS.
EVERYWHERE.
JOURNAL

Write it down. Check it off!

> "Love is always bestowed as a gift—freely, willingly, and without expectation. We don't love to be loved; we love to love.
>
> —DR. LEO F. BUSCAGLIA"

habit TRACKER

M T W T F S S

| JAN | FEB | MAR | APR | MAY | JUN | JUL | AUG | SEP | OCT | NOV | DEC |

1 2 3 4 5 6 7 8 9 10 11 12 13 14 15 16 17 18 19 20 21 22 23 24 25 26 27 28 29 30 31

monday

tuesday

wednesday

I correct and punish those whom I love. So be eager to do right, and change your hearts and lives.

REVELATION 3:19

thursday

friday

What's it mean?
TO ME THIS VERSE SAYS:

saturday / sunday

Instagram
@HEARTS.
EVERYWHERE.
JOURNAL

Write it down Check it off!

> "You can give without loving, but you can never love without giving."
>
> —ROBERT LOUIS STEVENSON

habit TRACKER — M T W T F S S

| JAN | FEB | MAR | APR | MAY | JUN | JUL | AUG | SEP | OCT | NOV | DEC |

1 2 3 4 5 6 7 8 9 10 11 12 13 14 15 16 17 18 19 20 21 22 23 24 25 26 27 28 29 30 31

About the Designer

Lela Rast Hartsaw is a writer, speaker, and historic preservationist living on Florida's Emerald Coast with her husband, two teens, and her 90-year-old father-in-law (a retired Navy Commander).

Intending to help save the 1895 Patten House (in jeopardy of being demolished in 2016), Lela published two children's books (_The Adventures of Abigail Rose—Ida Patten's Antebellum Doll_ and _Abigail Rose Visits Gamble Plantation_). The interwoven histories of the Patten House and its neighbor, the Gamble Mansion (built in 1850), are integral to the history of the local community, the state of Florida, and our nation.

In 2017, Lela published her third book, the story of her great grandparents, called _Remembering Lela & Charlie—A Four-Generation Book Project._ The project consisted of her grand-aunt's type-written memories of growing up in the rural south of early 20th century America. Mom did the research and editing. Then-13-year-old daughter drew the illustrations. Lela wrote the Introduction and Bonus Materials, designed and published the book. Since then, Lela also published two more books for her grand-aunt: _Remembering Lela & Charlie—The Blue Springs Years_ and a collection of short stories called _Home & Hearth—Southern Stories/Family Recipes._

These books are available on Amazon, as well as online through Barnes & Noble, Books-A-Million, Target, and WalMart.

Collecting photos of found hearts is one of Lela's hobbies and inspired this journal. Her photos, typically posted to Instagram and Facebook, are quite popular and have become something Lela is known for among her friends and followers. People now often find hearts and share them with her, which makes her smile.

About the Design

This journal was created on an iPad using the Canva app.

All photos were taken by the author using an iPhone and are property of the owner.

Fonts used: Apricots, Barlow Light, Big Shoulders Display, Cup Cakes, Horizon, Libre Franklin Black, Moontime, and Nickainley.

Made in United States
Orlando, FL
22 November 2022

24869964R00061